D0779885

SAYING *Thanks* AND *Beyond*

Is Saying Thank You Enough?

Ralph Mosgrove

Copyright © 2017 Ralph Mosgrove.

All rights reserved. No part of this book may be used or reproduced by any means, graphic, electronic, or mechanical, including photocopying, recording, taping or by any information storage retrieval system without the written permission of the author except in the case of brief quotations embodied in critical articles and reviews.

Archway Publishing books may be ordered through booksellers or by contacting:

Archway Publishing
1663 Liberty Drive
Bloomington, IN 47403
www.archwaypublishing.com
1 (888) 242-5904

Because of the dynamic nature of the Internet, any web addresses or links contained in this book may have changed since publication and may no longer be valid. The views expressed in this work are solely those of the author and do not necessarily reflect the views of the publisher, and the publisher hereby disclaims any responsibility for them.

Any people depicted in stock imagery provided by Thinkstock are models, and such images are being used for illustrative purposes only.
Certain stock imagery © Thinkstock.

ISBN: 978-1-4808-4352-3 (sc)
ISBN: 978-1-4808-4353-0 (e)

Library of Congress Control Number: 2017904335

Print information available on the last page.

Archway Publishing rev. date: 03/29/2017

Contents

Acknowledgments

There are so many family, friends, and acquaintances who have contributed to the reason this book has been written. My good friend, Timothy F. Wentworth, who first edited my manuscript; son, Reed, and wife, Lisa; grandsons, Ryan ad Kyle, who supported the writing; and those who stand out as contributors to making this story come alive. Friends like Sr. Dolores O'Brien, Barbara Lightfoot Tobey, Steve Santa-Cruz; from Christian Women's Connection, Clearwater, Florida, Stonecroft Ministries, Janet Hall, Meredith Lamb, Muriel Ice, and Ann Aderholdt; from Salvation Army, Major Georgia Henderson and Lena Gatto; the music department of MacDill AFB Chapel, Tampa, Florida, Fr. Juan Diphe, and choirs who extended kindness and a generous spirit, to the late Eileen Lightfoot, Freda Lau, and Rev. Doris Parker. To each of them and so many more, I say thank you.

Dedication

This book is dedicated to the memory of my wife, Rev. Elsie Louise (Meyer) Mosgrove, whose life epitomized *Saying Thanks and Beyond.*

Introduction

This book was birthed from the traumatic experiences of two elderly people who loved each other over sixty years of marriage. The tragedy we encountered caused us to reconsider the words we so often said to the host of generous people we encountered on our journey. "Thank you." Here we relay ways to go beyond those two words. Workingmen and workingwomen living in a high-tech society with a low-touch culture and young adults fashioning lifestyles for themselves will find ways to brighten the lives of others, encouraging them to actively share life that not only brings inner satisfaction but causes others to want to go beyond as well. You will find anecdotes along the way to open your mind to new possibilities. You will discover ways you can incorporate ideas into your daily habits you never thought of before.

My late wife, Elsie, became disabled when she took a major fall at the age of seventy-seven.

She broke her right hip, which was repaired with a partial hip replacement, and had two compression fractures of the vertebra at T12 and L1. Vertebroplasty was used to strengthen the bones and stabilize her so she could get around using a walker. That fall changed everything for both of us over the next eight years, until her death. After trying several models of walkers—from aluminum sliders to three-wheel, triangular-shaped ones—she settled on a four-wheel walker with a seat on it. She was unable to manipulate any of them by herself, and although she could still drive, someone had to be with her to load and unload the walker from the car.

It was an abrupt interruption to our committed lives. Although we were both retired from our careers, she in social work and I as a pastor, we pursued other means of staying productive and engaged. She took part in the leadership of Christian Women's Ministries, worked as weekend receptionist at Bon Secours Assisted Living Facility, and participated in senior programs at local churches. I was organist and choir director for MacDill AFB Chapel, in Tampa, Florida, for Protestant and Catholic worship. The trauma affected both of us as our whole lives stopped, and we tried to work out the adjustments necessary for her well-being.

Whenever we headed for the door of a local store, shopping or walking at the mall, we would meet someone approaching the door at the same time. The person would take his or her time to open it and allow her to go in first. I was there, ready to open the door, but the other person wanted to do something for a disabled person and freely gave of himself or herself on our behalf. It was not required and certainly unexpected, but we often commented on the courtesy. But how do you say more than, "Thank you?"

Eight years after her fall, Elsie died in April 2015 at the age of eighty-three. I had time to put some thoughts together on ways to say thanks and beyond, which led to writing this book. Here I explore ways to acknowledge those people who have demonstrated kindness, generosity, patience, and self-denial. You know who you are, and you should be honored for your actions. I believe whoever reads this book will be inspired to do those good deeds and promote such character in others who never gave it any thought.

Copies of this book can become a gift to hand out when you want to say, "Thank you," to a friend, a business associate, a speaker at your social club, for a special day at church, like Father's Day or Mother's Day celebrations. Here's a way to answer the question, "Is saying thank you enough?" This book takes you beyond those words, "Thank you." And what might have been a routine day becomes a day filled with joy and satisfaction. Gratitude begets gratitude. What you feel is expressed through your words that, in turn, attracts more happy experiences. Your inner self stretches to higher levels of exchange with those around you. You find your full potential and growth as a human being by accepting the gift and responding with "Thank you."

Part of going beyond is imparting grace and kindness to persons you thank, making them glad they took the time to be gracious. They are inspired to do it again, and you encouraged it by your "Thank you."

The Ripple Effect: How Have You Observed This Effect?

Our words have the power to bring life or death. When I use words that bring positive feelings, it means I am on the right track.

When you throw a stone into a pond, the impact sends out circular ripples to the far reaches of the water's boundaries and returns to the point of contact. They tell us the same is true of our brains. We emit brain waves, rippling through space and measured by instruments to detect if we are alive.

From my earliest days of childhood, I have used the words "Thank you" as my mother taught me. Without conscious thought, a pattern of ripples began forming, carrying my message to those around me. I carried that phrase into adulthood. The vibration set in motion from the spoken word gives the same reaction regardless of what the words are. Our words have the power to bring life or death. When I use words that bring positive feelings, it means I am on the right track. The same is true of negative statements. Using words that bring out bad feelings means I am on the wrong track. When

I say, "Thank you," it is an expression spoken to someone who extends himself or herself to give me assistance along my journey. They absorb the ripples as though being soaked up and penetrated with good feelings. I have been thinking about this simple phrase that is so quickly used and often without real meaning. Saying thank you is an opportunity to let someone know how much you really appreciated the person's generous and friendly act. As the recipient of a "Thank you," you know how it makes you feel. That's why you pass it on, impacting a person you may never see again.

There are many ways to say, "Thank you," and learning ways it can be done is something most of us have given little thought to. Some make it sound like a military statement. Crisp and precise. When a young woman is given an engagement ring, you can be sure it is emotional and full of feelings. Joyful, excited, and exuberant. Her heart is full of love and gratitude for the man who has set her apart. She's spoken for. It makes a young man smile all over. Or what about the child who gets that special Christmas gift ordered from Santa, with yelps and shouts of, "Thank you, thank you, thank you," heard throughout the two-story house.

After years of using the phrase, it occurs to me there are certain occasions calling for a more genuine response, especially as you approach a door when you are disadvantaged, disabled with arms full, or with small children to attend to. It's like receiving a gift of friendship, evoking a smile, or a spoken word of encouragement. They say, "Let me get that door for you." They stand there patiently as a quiet sentinel, passing on the gift they received earlier, letting ripple effects carry the gift forward.

Sometimes you encounter someone who is not as compassionate or understanding of your dilemma and hastens his or her step to get out of your way. There is no way of knowing why the response is so feeble, but you keep the right attitude, even if the conduct appears to be self-centered. When you feel a negative impulse toward that person, you come to a choice in your thought process. What you think about a person can determine your feelings. If you respond negatively, think, *He must have had a bad experience since he didn't see that I might need his help.* Your attitude is taking shape, and you fight off the negativity because it only detracts from who you are. Instead, you keep the right attitude and realize that person may be distracted because of a personal crisis and just missed an opportunity to show a moment of kindness. After all, the world does not revolve around you. We never know what others face in their lives. The thoughts you focus on effect your feelings, and feelings attract the kind of experiences you have.

Speak Up: See What Benefits Come to You When You Speak Up.

Whatever you send out, comes back to you
in the same way.

You might ask if this concern for gratitude is necessary. I can assure you it is! How can the person offering help know how much you appreciate what he or she did for you if you don't speak words of affirmation? There are several reasons for saying this. Let me give you some details on why.

Speaking up, giving verbal assent, provides active responses to what you say. Your words have the power to lift one up or, unfortunately, put someone down. Remember how you felt when you didn't get accolades from the boss after you put in that extra effort and stayed late to complete a job? There was no favorable response for your contribution. You made a mental note, wondering if you were as forthcoming in praises to others as you expect them to be with you. There is a time for silence and a time for speaking. Saying thank you creates a positive reaction in the mind of the person spoken to. Speaking words of encouragement generates what comes back to you. You are the magnet that draws in the response of kindness.

The story is told of a little boy who was playing in a meadow surrounded by a thick forest. He was lonely and called out for anyone to come join him in his play. Much to his surprise, he heard a voice returning his call from beyond in the woods. Curious, he called, “Hello, is someone there?” And the woods answered with his own words. He repeated the call with different phrases, like, “Who are you?” or, “Come out and play with me.” Each time he got an answer using the same phrase. Upset, he went home and told his mother of the boy in the woods, making fun of him. Mother explained what he was hearing was his own voice. “Your voice bounces off the trees and echoes back to you.” Whatever you send out, comes back to you in the same way. If you send out angry words or mean-spirited comments, they will come back just the way you sent them. That’s why it is important to say, “Thank you,” whenever you can; it will be returned. It’s a loop that goes around to you, always coming back in the form in which it was expressed.

I observed a young couple in the grocery store doing their rounds by going in the opposite direction from most of the shoppers. Ultimately, they met face to face with an old woman using a walker. On more than one occasion, there was confrontation for the same space. They pushed their way in, reaching in front of the older person, and making disgruntled sounds as if to say, "You're in the way!" Never a polite phrase like, "Excuse me," or, "Can I help you find something." When you receive an act of kindness, it makes you want to say thank you and seek opportunities to extend the same courtesy to someone else.

There are also other ways of saying thanks. Send a handwritten note to the hostess who invited you for coffee or someone who did something kind for you. Now that's a novel idea! You might even go so far as to offer a small gift of thanks by taking some used books to the neighbor's children when you go to a dinner party next door.

I have determined that saying, "Thank you," is often an idle response to someone's concern or desire to help. There is a way to offer a response that shows your appreciation for kind deeds, exceeding what others would expect. For example, what if we were to add phrases such as, "That was such a big help," or, "You certainly made that easy for me." When you tell someone, "You made my day," he or she feels good about helping you and leaves with a smile or feeling of satisfaction. We all have an arsenal of comments we could use to express our gratitude to individuals extending this helping hand. Try telling them how much you needed their help, like, "I couldn't have made it without you," or, "Someday it will come back to you." You reinforce their spirits of generosity, helping them to keep passing it on.

I would like to take it even further by exhibiting other traits of kindness, goodness, patience, faithfulness, meekness, self-control, and even love, joy, and peace. What would you get if you studied these words, analyzed them, and applied them to your daily routine? Would the practice become an extension of the words "Thank you"? Perhaps it would be the means of passing forward the gracious act you received. The person who was kind would not know what you have done, but rewards come back to him or her from other avenues as an echo. That would be awesome!

Let's look at the word "kindness." A broad search of this word from the ancient Greek includes "excellent," "serviceable," "useful," "adapted to its purpose," "decent," and "honest" as defining words. There is nothing in that interpretation that cannot be passed on. In fact, it is evident that the person performing the kindness is motivated by an inner sense of what is decent and good. When I say, "Thank you," with that attitude, I am inspired to make it an act of kindness of my own, extending it into the future.

Kindness is not always received in the same way by everyone. When handouts are given to people less fortunate than you, it can lead to pride for a giver who wants to be seen as a caring person. It can also allow someone to be lazy. Such individuals may think because their resources are limited, they're not able to process life as others do. They lose their motivation. When the receiver reflects a sure sign of ingratitude, you know the person is thinking primarily of himself or herself and not those who really need the help. You can be kind to one, and that individual will show gratitude; someone else may respond as being ungrateful.

Personal Reflection

It's Better to Give Than Receive.

True gratitude comes from the heart, and the lips serve as the messenger.

If giving is really in the best interest of the person, you give without taking credit and without recognition. You are bearing each other's burdens along the way. You have become your brother's keeper with no expectations in return. That person who opened the door is the only one who can know the real motive for giving. If it is seen by people passing by or used as self-aggrandizement, then whatever adulation you receive is your only reward. The attitude, "Look at me," or, "See what I am doing," does not result in positive thoughts. God knows all things, and if it was done for others, God gives the reward. Otherwise, a word of thanks is all you get. True gratitude comes from the heart, and the lips serve as the messenger. Giving from the heart means you are doing something good for a person in need, and that produces positive results.

Howard hired a chauffeur, Mark, to drive him around. The man was without a job, and Howard wanted to do something to help him out. After three episodes of careless driving, putting his life in danger, Howard questioned Mark's ability as a driver. He complained to his wife, saying, "I think the chauffer is trying to kill me." He told her he was going to fire Mark for putting him in danger. She earnestly asked him to give Mark one more chance. Howard decided to give Mark another chance as driver and talked to him about his driving skills. Speaking up gave both parties a chance to make corrections in thoughts and action. They agreed Mark needed additional training, so Howard paid for Mark to take lessons, which proved beneficial to both. Mark became a valued chauffer and loyal employee for a long time. It was also discovered that the car Howard rode in was too small for the long-legged Mark, so it was traded for a larger one with more leg room, giving Mark the needed space for safe driving. Mark was grateful for the job and demonstrated his thanks to Howard for the job and for the opportunities opened to him. He went beyond saying, "Thank you," by the way he drove and cared for the car. Howard found a new level of satisfaction, too, when he went beyond the criticism.

He realized negative thoughts cause more negative results. Mark was able to be a chauffeur through the generosity of Howard, who rejected the negative attitude for a positive one.

Personal Reflection

Adapted to Its Purpose: A Call to Make a Deliberate Choice.

You have to want to do good before you are good. It comes from a spiritual base, acquired, not developed.

Being kind to others is not second nature to any of us. We are naturally inclined to be self-centered and want our own way. Kindness is a learned activity. It is a choice we make based on early training and past experiences. We are ready to step forward to show kindness when we see a need. We all experience the true meaning of the Greek definition of kindness.

Being adapted to its purpose is a good indicator that we are doing what we were created to do—maintaining those God-given graces taught to us in our childhood. Gentleness is closely related to kindness, but there is a distinction to be acknowledged. When you see someone frail and struggling, you move in to give the person a little support. Being aware of your surroundings often shows us ways to be kind and gentle with others. Marge is a good example.

She noticed the elderly man struggle with the grocery bag he thought he could carry to the car. She very gently approached him so as not to embarrass him, and said, "Here, let me help you with that heavy bag." And before he had time to object, the deed was done. She walked him to his car and put the groceries inside. It was a deliberate choice to give herself to someone else because she had been the recipient of such acts of kindness.

I was waiting in the doctor's office when a mother with two children came in. The receptionist gave the mother some papers to complete before seeing the doctor. There was a gentle soul sitting close by and immediately saw the problem with Mom's struggle to balance two babies and complete the forms. The woman asked the mother, "Can I help with the children?" Gentleness is the ability to be useful to others in a way that puts them at ease. Gentleness is not an aggressive attitude but, rather, mild mannered and courteous. It is an answer to a call to make a deliberate choice.

There is a close relationship between the characteristics of kindness, gentleness, and goodness. Goodness, however, is born out of kindness and being useful (gentle). People do good deeds all the time because they have perfected their attitudes toward others. They have purposed in their life to be good to others. This characteristic is not a given. You have to want to do good before you are good. It comes from a spiritual base, acquired, not developed. Goodness is a quality that is endowed by the supernatural. God, Himself, gives it to us. We have the choice to use or lose it. You join the ranks of the unidentified secret agents of God, going about doing good wherever you can. You not only have this feeling of exuberance, knowing what you have done, but the person to whom you've been good to receives confidence that inspires him or her to do the same for someone else. It creates a chain reaction that continues into the eons of time. It is formed in kindness and reveals traits beneficial to others. We become perfected in our attitudes, causing us to give of ourselves and to find ways to build up someone else who needs a lift in spirit. Jane was such a person when she came upon a couple in the middle of an emergency.

Marty and Marie were hiking on the mountain trail when Marie stepped on a rock that threw her off balance. Twisting her ankle, she fell off the path, down a slope, and hit a tree, breaking her arm on impact. Marty was so distraught he couldn't think straight. He tried to call 911 but was out of range when Jane and her German shepherd came along the trail and found them. She left her dog with the couple for comfort and headed down the path until she could make the call for emergency help. Marie got the medical attention she needed, and they were safely off the mountain. Jane's goodness saved their lives. It is that quality of serving another person in need of encouragement. Yes, it borders on kindness and gentleness, but doing a good deed goes beyond the limits of kindness and being useful. This is a willing act of giving of self out of a natural sense of doing what is good and right!

Demonstrating acts of kindness, being gentle toward others, and responding to less fortunate out of the goodness of your heart are all ways of passing on the thank you that lurks inside until you find completion in the meaning of those two words. You may not be able to say it to the person who first showed kindness in helping you, but this is a way to encourage someone's life along the way as you part company. It is going beyond saying, "Thank you."

Hands and Feet: What Response Do You Get from Your Body Language?

Facial expressions can cause reactions for good and bad.

When you want to express thank you for someone's act of kindness, say it with your hands, your feet, your heart, and especially with your face! A smile carries a huge message. Our body language evokes many responses. In the Asian community, I observed their habit of bowing to each other. It is a sign of respect and recognition, letting you know they are aware of your presence, and you are welcome. Facial expressions can cause reactions for good and bad. You know from the countenance of someone whether he or she sees you in a favorable light or are unhappy with you. I have to go back to an age when my mother gave me a certain look, and I knew exactly what she meant. She didn't have to speak a word. I had better shape up, or I would hear about it when I got home. When you read someone's body language, you are seeing into the inner core of the person's being. You notice the ability they have to inspire another to conform to their expectations. You believe that the person receiving your attention will take notice of your favor, accept it in good faith, and go on to show gratitude for your kindness. That's where "Loving your neighbor as yourself" comes to play; treating others as you would like to be treated. Think about it. How powerful is that in thought, word, and deed?

It was most interesting to watch the reaction of family members who witnessed their father holding the door for the needy person. What a lesson learned from a slice of life without knowing it. Mom said to her husband, "Did you see the lady's facial expression when you held the door for her? She had a look of such appreciation." The children, standing by, heard Mom's comments and held them in the secret places of their hearts for safekeeping until they, too, someday put them to use. They will follow Dad's example and feel the same warm, inner glow of satisfaction. You've gone over and above what is expected, while others miss the possibilities, failing to see the good.

My wife and I were waiting in the doctor's office when a mother came out of the examining room with a stroller and a toddler in tow. A young boy, about ten years old, jumped up and took charge of the door to assist the mother as she left the office. We later commented about his performance and thought, *Now there's an example of good training in the home.*

Personal Reflection

Side Effects: Characteristics that Complement Each Other.

You never lose when you go beyond the expectations of those around you.

Being a doorkeeper to the less fortunate and needy takes on the side effects of humility, long-suffering, tolerance, meekness, and self-control. The one who takes on that role is an ambassador of goodwill. When I have encountered similar situations, it was never in my plan for the day. I saw a need and determined to help resolve it. It required patience to allow someone to pass in front of me through the door I was about to enter. To stand there, holding the door for the person in need, often takes on other bystanders wanting to get inside, too. Patience is being tolerant of others when you do not have to. When a negative attitude is displayed, you can counteract it by responding with a comment that changes the atmosphere of the situation. There are those who do not want others to get in front of them. They may hold the door for someone and then maneuver their bodies directly behind them to prevent others from entering because of their courteous acts. That's not patience. Even in that circumstance, you can offer your own words of thanks while they hold the door for you. Show an attitude of servanthood by saying, "Let me hold that for you." Say something that disarms them and puts them in a better frame of mind. It is never wasted effort. It comes back to you from sources you may never see or be aware of. Patience leads to self-control. When people humble themselves to the point of preferring others first, they demonstrate the power of meekness, not weakness. There is an inner strength that bears influence by promoting the other person before yourself. Taking the backseat may look like you are missing out on an opportunity, and someone else will get the promotion or the sale item you wanted. After many attempts to push ahead, I've learned the few seconds gained do not measure up to the feeling of satisfaction when you realize you have enabled another person to excel in his or her venture. You never lose when you go beyond the expectations of those around you. They notice, and they add value to your life when you are not looking. That's having it come back to you. If it is meant for you, it will come to you in due season. Saying thanks and beyond has so many possibilities. It is never enough to just say, "Thank you." Look around, find a way to enter into what's beyond, and see what benefits you gain.

Becoming a friendly face, you inherit the characteristics found in gifts given to us by the Almighty. Some of us use them profusely, and others resist the impulse. When you embrace such qualities, you demonstrate divine principles that do not go unnoticed—not only by God, but by others as well. Going beyond teaches unspoken lessons that become patterns for living, qualities of life, and habits that expose a deeper sense of what it means to answer the question, "Is saying thank you enough?"